Patches of Inspiration™

Harvesting Your Success

By

Sonie Bigbee

Published by

Queen V Publishing
Dayton, Ohio
QueenVPublishing.net

Published by

Queen V Publishing
Dayton, Ohio
QueenVPublishing.net
Info@PenoftheWriter.com

Copyright © 2008 by S. Bigbee.

Patches of Inspiration™ is a registered trademark of Patches of Inspiration, LLC
PatchesofInspiration.com

All rights reserved. No part of this book may be reproduced or transmitted in any form or by any means, electronic or mechanical, without prior written consent of the Publisher, except for the inclusion of brief quotes in a review.

Queen V Publishing is a Christian contract publishing company of standard and integrity. We allow God's Word in you to do what it was sent to do for others.

Library of Congress Control Number: 2008936915

ISBN-13: 978-0-9817436-2-2

Cover design by Candace K
Edited by Valerie L. Coleman of PenoftheWriter.com

Printed in the United States of America

Scripture quotations marked KJV are taken from the King James Version of the Bible.

Scripture quotations marked NIV are taken from the Holy Bible, New International Version®. NIV®. Copyright © 1973, 1978, 1984 by International by International Bible Society. Used by permission of Zondervan. All rights reserved.

Scripture quotations marked NASB are taken from the New American Standard Bible, Copyright © 1960, 1962, 1963, 1968, 1971, 1972, 1973, 1975, 1977, 1995 by the Lockman Foundation. Used by permission.

Scripture quotations marked NKJV are taken from the New King James Version®. Copyright © 1982 by Thomas Nelson, Inc. Used by permission. All rights reserved.

Scripture quotations marked NLT are taken from the *Holy Bible,* New Living Translation, Copyright © 1996. Used by permission of Tyndale House Publishers, Inc. Wheaton, Illinois 60189, U.S.A. All rights reserved.

Scripture quotations marked HCSB are taken from the Holman Christian Standard Bible®, Copyright © 1999, 2000, 2002, 2003 by Holman Bible Publishers. Used by permission. Holman Christian Standard Bible®, Holman CSB® and HCSB® are federally registered trademarks of Holman Bible Publishers.

Dedication

This book is dedicated to my Lord and Savior, Jesus Christ, who has given me the strength, desire and talent to write this book.

Acknowledgements

I would especially like to thank God, my Lord and Savior.

To my family, I love each and every one of you. Thank you for all that you do. You keep me whole and have a special place in my heart. My life experiences have grown deeper and I am a better woman because of you.

To everyone who has played a role in my spiritual growth and development, thank you for your teachings and prayers.

To my friends, thank you for being a part of my support circle.

Table of Contents

Introduction 11
Patches Principles 13
   Is It a Seed, Root or Weed? 13
Make a Spiritual Connection 15
What is Meant for You is for You 28
The Power of Leadership and Action 32
Does Your Image Work? 48
The Meaningful Network and Environment 56
Courage to Maneuver Obstacles and Challenges 63
State of Mind 72
Owning Goals, Understanding Opportunity 80
Align Your Pursuit with Your Priorities 91
Failure is Not So Bad 100
Harvest Study Guide 107

Patches of Inspiration ^{TM} Success Model 134
About Sonie Bigbee 135
Queen V Publishing 136

Plant seeds that will yield a lifetime of harvest.

Introduction

For quite some time, I have wanted to inspire others and make a difference in the world. I am so proud that I can begin that mission with this book. I have spent several years navigating obstacles and challenges. Spending a significant amount of my professional career in sales positions for Fortune 500 companies, my professional experience has been about setting and achieving goals. I worked through some unique experiences including being one of the first women to have ownership interest in a professional sports franchise.

I have had the privilege of mentorship by great professionals and I have taken those lessons to coach others to success. In the *Patches of Inspiration*™ series, I share principles that can be used in your professional and personal endeavors. Application of this information will master your gardening skills as you learn to seed, root and weed your way to success. My hope is that you reap a harvest of bountiful blessings.

Sonie Bigbee

Sonie Bigbee

Patches Principles
Is It a Seed, Root or Weed?

Understanding the seeds, roots and weeds in your life is important. Through this process, you learn how to prioritize and focus on the things that matter most.

Seeds represent something that needs to be planted to achieve goals. Roots are symbolic of things that you want to nourish, grow and develop. Weeds represent obstacles that you need to remove. Just as weeds serve no purpose in your yard and need to be plucked up, they have no place in your life and need to be uprooted.

As in agriculture, successful harvesting starts with planting good seeds in fertile soil. Whatever and wherever we root is critical to the outcome. Identification of roots and providing the appropriate nourishment keeps dreams alive. Removing weeds — hindering individuals and circumstances — we minimize failure and destruction. Implementing this process creates perpetual growth.

For seven days celebrate the Feast to the Lord your God at the place the Lord will choose. For the Lord your God will bless you in all your harvest and in all the work of your hands, and your joy will be complete.

~ Deuteronomy 16:15 NIV

Remember this—a farmer who plants only a few seeds will get a small crop. But the one who plants generously will get a generous crop.

~ II Corinthian 9:6 NLT

Make a Spiritual Connection

Spiritual connection, which is both a seed and root, is essential to your success. Because God is intertwined in every aspect of your journey the spiritual seed needs constant planting and nourishment. Luke, a disciple and physician, illustrated the importance of seeds, planting and harvesting in his biblical writings. The parable of tares, found in Luke 8, discusses the affects of a farmer who scattered seeds in various types of soil. Some seeds fell on a footpath and were eaten by birds. Some seeds fell among rocks and thorns. The lack of moisture created fallow ground impenetrable by the seeds. As a result, the seeds could not take root and died. The remaining seeds fell on fertile soil. They grew and produced crops a hundred times more than what was planted.

Every aspect of your spiritual relationship will have a direct impact on your inspiration and success. God has ordained how He wants us to live. Through relationship and understanding His expectations, God will bless us beyond anything imaginable.

> *Inspiration Patch*
> *Life without a spiritual core is a hollow shell.*

A core is the innermost part of an object. Your core is the most important part of you and should be filled with the Spirit of God. However, without much effort, we fill our lives with relationships, money, material possessions and jobs. The space allocated for God is occupied with things that do not fulfill or sustain us. For this reason, people who appear to have it all can be hollow because they have not filled themselves with substance.

Dear friend, I hope all is well with you and that you are as healthy in body as you are strong in spirit.
~ III John 1:2 NLT

> *Inspiration Patch*
> *If you want something, ask God.*

When we want something, we tend to ask for it from the person whom we believe is in control; the authority. A child will ask permission from his mother when he wants a cookie. If an employee wants a raise, she asks her boss.

The ultimate question is who is in control? God is! He controls all. Stop asking people who have selective control and ask the one who is in ultimate control. God's consultations and requests are free and fulfilling.

But if you remain in Me and My words remain in you, you may ask for anything you want, and it will be granted!
~ John 15:7 NLT

Inspiration Patch
You can have what you want because God fulfills the desires of your heart.

Several Scriptures share God's blessings to others. The key is to ask. Let God know what you want for your life. He promised that through relationship with Him, He will give us what we ask. With our belief in God, we can have everything we desire.

And whatever things you ask in prayer, believing, you will receive.
~ Matthew 21:22 NKJV

> **Inspiration Patch**
> *God opens the doors that seem impossible to unlock.*

At times, the world says "no," but God can say "yes." During trying situations, we see God's power at work and witness the beauty of being His children. God lets us know that we can have all things that are in His will; even those things that seem out of reach. Life's doors are opened with keys of blessings given to us from God.

> *Ask, and it will be given to you; seek, and you will find; knock, and it will be opened to you.*
> ~ Matthew 7:7 NKJV

> **Inspiration Patch**
> *Prayer is the most important conversation you can have.*

Power resides in prayer, your 800 number to heaven. Scripture tells us how God answers prayer with heavenly miracles that manifest on earth. Communication is the single most important aspect of any relationship and this principle applies with God. Both inspiration and success come through our relationship with Christ; a relationship built on prayer. Inspiration comes in knowing that through a conversation with God, we have the power to unlock the blessings of heaven.

I will answer them before they even call to Me. While they are still talking about their needs, I will go ahead and answer their prayers!
~ Isaiah 65:24 NLT

Inspiration Patch
Worry is living without faith.

We need a huge dose of faith. National and local tragedies can leave us feeling helpless and hopeless. Worry is another word for handicap because limited thinking doubts the ability of divine intervention. We need faith to believe that whatever we pursue or endure; a power greater than anything on earth has our best interest at heart. We need to learn to let go and let God and trust that He has it under control.

So don't worry about these things, saying, 'What will we eat? What will we drink? What will we wear?' These things dominate the thoughts of unbelievers, but your heavenly Father already knows all your needs.

~ Matthew 6:31-32 NLT

What do we need to do?

Seek the Kingdom of God above all else, and live righteously, and He will give you everything you need.

~ Matthew 6:33 NLT

Inspiration Patch
Divine intervention paves the way for things to fall into place.

Divine intervention is destiny's way of stepping in to take control of life's situations. Your destiny is greatness and all things will work out for your greater good. Affirm this conviction and you open the door to destiny.

Like a plane on autopilot, destiny will take its course. With the push of a button, the pilot can shift control from manual to automatic. Although he is still in the cockpit observing and monitoring the situation, he has relinquished control. I am a firm believer in auto pilot. If you have to work too hard at something, question if you are in manual

Patches of Inspiration™ - Harvesting Your Success

mode — following selfish desires — or autopilot — God's will. What God has for you, is for you. Pray that His will aligns with the desires of your heart, then let destiny fly you to your appointed destination.

> *But I am trusting You, O LORD, saying, "You are my God!"*
> ~ Psalm 31:14 NLT

Inspiration Patch
Wisdom is knowledge that blesses your life.

Strive for wisdom. With the advent of the Internet, knowledge is readily available, however only the wise can effectively apply it. Intelligent decision-making separates success from failure.

Wisdom also provides a sense of good judgment: the ability to use awareness to make an assessment. Understanding acquired information we can make informed decisions and optimize our quality of life.

> *How much better to get wisdom than gold, and good judgment than silver!*
> ~ Proverbs 16:16 NLT

> *Inspiration Patch*
> *God gives us gifts and talents. Through this ability, we fulfill our purpose and achieve success.*

> *Inspiration Patch*
> *The thing you do best is your gift.*

Stop trying to figure out what you want to do and figure out what you are supposed to do. We set out on our own missions and desires. Life is not about our mission, but God's mission for us. You have a special gift or talent that exudes from you without much effort. Has anyone ever said to you, "You are a natural at _____"? More than likely, that's your gift. Trust your talents and let your gifts flow. God placed them in you for a reason. Walk in purpose to achieve your greatest rewards. Note that success is not about stacking up material possessions, but generating purpose and peace.

Beautiful voices and apt musical abilities amaze me. When I learn that artists do not desire to function in their gifts, disappointment ensues. God showers us with gifts and pleasures when we ask, "Father, what do You want me to do?"

Patches of Inspiration™ - Harvesting Your Success

Taking our talent for granted is easy. Working to fulfill God's plan takes commitment and focus. The key to your happiness, wealth and eternal peace could be laying dormant inside of you.

> *God has given each of you a gift from His great variety of spiritual gifts. Use them well to serve one another.*
> ~ I Peter 4:10 NLT

Inspiration Patch
Peace is found through the spirit in you.

Peace cannot be bought or borrowed from others. It comes from within and fulfilled by only God and you. Meditate and pray daily that you have a spirit of peace.

> *For God has not given us a spirit of fear and timidity, but of power, love and self-discipline.*
> ~ II Timothy 1:7 NLT

Inspiration Patch
A compassionate hand gives love.

Compassion is sympathetic concern for others. Love is affection for others. Strive for both. Through sympathetic concern, great works of charity are executed resulting in acts of love. Since God blesses the giver, success rests in giving.

> *They share freely and give generously to those in need. Their good deeds will be remembered forever. They will have influence and honor.*
> ~ Psalm 112:9 NLT

> *You must each decide in your heart how much to give. And don't give reluctantly or in response to pressure. For God loves a person who gives cheerfully.*
> ~ II Corinthian 9:7 NLT

Inspiration Patch
By helping others today, you create tomorrow's blessings.

Through our experiences and blessings, we can guide others. Anytime you have the opportunity to help others do it gladly. These acts of kindness open doors to our blessings.

Patches of Inspiration™ - Harvesting Your Success

People remember what you do for them more than what you do for yourself. If you want to leave a legacy, be known as someone that helped others and the good news will spread to others.

> *Give, and you will receive. Your gift will return to you in full—pressed down, shaken together to make room for more, running over, and poured into your lap. The amount you give will determine the amount you get back.*
> ~ Luke 6:38 NLT

Inspiration Patch
Use your blessings to encourage others.

You are a vehicle to demonstrate God's blessings. At every opportunity, stand and let the world know what God has done for you. Through this boastful display of gratitude, you create an opportunity to encourage others. Encouragement is not only what you say; it also involves what you display. "Seeing is believing."

All must give as they are able, according to the blessings given to them by the LORD your God.
~ Deuteronomy 16:17

Create a Spiritual Harvest

Seed: Something you need
- Relationship with God
- Wisdom
- Knowledge
- Faith
- Prayer
- Peace

Root: Something you need to grow and develop
- Relationship with God
- Faith
- Gifts
- Talents
- Life's purpose
- Prayer
- Giving

Weed: Something you need to remove
- Worry
- Doubt
- Evil spirits
- Ignorance

Notes _____
_____
_____
_____
_____
_____

What is Meant for You is for You

The destiny patch falls into the root category. Living in destiny requires frequent use and nurturing of gifts and talents. Fulfillment has a story of greatness, fullness and prosperity for you.

Many people doubt that something remarkable is meant for them and they erect a roadblock in destiny's path. While utilizing your gifts and talents, nothing and no one can stop what is meant for you.

Inspiration Patch
Fate happens naturally. People fulfill life's destiny.

Fate is uncontrollable. No matter what we say or do our fate will come to pass. Destiny, the inevitable pre-determined course of events, is a series of actionable life experiences. Notice "pre-determined course of events." Are your affiliations and actions leading to success? If not, then get on the path to success.

> **Inspiration Patch**
> *Every person begins life with a purpose. Those that find and fulfill their purpose, accomplish greatness.*

For some, finding life's purpose comes quickly and without question. For others, the task can be difficult, daunting and burdensome. If you need a mission, let understanding and living in your purpose be your objective.

Purpose equates to a reason for existence which leads to justification for placement. Organized, planned, methodical placement minimizes chaos and clutter.

As you know, the purpose of a fork and glass are to eat and drink, respectively. Try using a fork to drink a cup of milk. The task is not impossible, but a lot of time, energy and milk will be wasted in the process. However, when the appropriate tools—talents—are used as intended, they serve their purpose. The result is victory.

When we live in our purpose, we achieve harmony and great rewards. Strive daily to live in your purpose.

> *But let each one examine his own work, and then he will have rejoicing in himself alone, and not in another. For each one shall bear his own load.*
> ~ Galatians 6:4-5 NKJV

> *Inspiration Patch*
> *A voice speaks to you daily. Listen; it guides your path.*

The inner voice, the core of a person, is a powerful source of guidance. The mind and inner voice may send conflicting messages. However, learn to listen to the inner voice as it is the door to life's success.

Over time, many things have been said about the inner voice. Many successful people have said that they followed their intuition or instinct. In other words, they followed their inner voice.

Tune in to your inner voice. Allow the core of your being to be the core of life's path. Let it speak to everything that you do.

> *The Lord directs the steps of the godly. He delights in every detail of their lives.*
> ~ Psalm 37:23 NLT

> *For I know the thoughts that I think toward you, saith the Lord; thoughts of peace, and not of evil, to give you an expected end.*
> ~ Jeremiah 29:11

Create a Destiny Harvest

Seed: Something you need
- Believe in your destiny
- Know your life's purpose
- Sensitivity to your inner voice

Root: Something you need to grow and develop
- Exercise your natural gifts and talents
- Listen to your inner voice
- Act in your purpose

Weed: Something you need to remove
- Activities that are not in your purpose
- Not using your gifts and talents

Notes _____

_____

_____

_____

_____

_____

_____

_____

_____

_____

_____

_____

The Power of Leadership and Action

The leadership patch is a seed and root because it must be planted and developed. Leadership is both a noun and verb as it describes who you are and what you do. Effective leadership requires a person to have an image that reflects the guidance given. The do-as-I-say-not-as-I-do philosophy trivializes the otherwise powerful position.

> *Inspiration Patch*
> *Some people make things happen, while others sit on the sidelines to watch things happen. The people who participate in the game achieve victory and reward.*

Are you a spectator or a participant? Can a team celebrate victory without playing the game? Of course not! You have to play to win. Life is about having a game plan, or strategy, to achieve your goals. If the world is the playing field, then coaches are mentors and teammates are resources to assist you.

Suit up and get on the field. Find the elements that will contribute to your success: coaches, teammates and the right playing field. Positioning yourself on the right playing field is just as important as the selection of coaches and teammates. A pitcher does not show up at a basketball court for a baseball game. Leaders positioned in the right environment achieve goals. If you want to be a brain surgeon, get in the medical industry. If your goal is entrepreneurship, get involved in small business associations.

Here is your game plan for life:

- Get in the game. Position yourself on the right playing field.
- Get the right coach. Identify mentors.
- Build your team. Find resources.
- Play to win. Create and execute a strategy.

Lazy people don't even cook the game they catch, but the diligent make use of everything they find.
~ Proverbs 12:27 NLT

Inspiration Patch
The choices made today impact tomorrow. Good choices lead to accomplishment, bad choices lead to frustration.

In addition to fate and destiny, life is about choices. In other words, I have the power to choose what I say, what I do, who I am and who I become.

Success and failure are choices. Most people who fail will probably not admit that they made the choice to fail because they do not see it. However, dissecting daily actions, will lead to the root of their decision.

Giving up on education or tolerating negative circumstances, is choosing to fail. Although bad choices can led to failure, it is not too late to opt for change. What you did yesterday affected today, and what you do today will affect tomorrow.

> *Commit yourself to instruction; listen carefully to words of knowledge.*
> ~ Proverbs 23:12 NLT

Inspiration Patch
Motivate yourself to do better than yesterday.

Aspire to do better. Confront each day with more experience and knowledge than the day before. Take your new growth as enhancements to excel to the next level.

Patches of Inspiration™ - Harvesting Your Success

Lazy people want much but get little, but those who work hard will prosper.

~ Proverbs 13:4 NLT

Inspiration Patch
Start tomorrow's victories with missions today.

Truth be told, most of us have been guilty of procrastination. The notorious push back is dieting. "I am going to go on my diet after I eat this cupcake." No! Everything that you do today is your tomorrow. What are you waiting for? Make things happen now. When you wake, say to yourself, "What can I do today that will contribute to the goals I have for tomorrow?" Don't put your life in a non-progressive cycle of status quo. Completing activities that contribute towards your goals is your daily quest.

Inspiration Patch
Dreams without action are memories lost.

The theme throughout this book is that desire contributes to making things happen. Many of us have dreams; idealistic fantasies that captivate our thoughts and minds. For years, I dreamt of speaking to large audiences and publishing a book. Since I have put action to my dreams, they have become my reality.

Dreams keep us going everyday. The thought of having or being something else is mesmerizing. Motivation and fantasies are good, but without action, they become a waste of time. When action is applied to dreams, they come to life and create memories for reflection.

> *So we do not focus on what is seen, but on what is unseen; for what is seen is temporary, but what is unseen is eternal.*
> ~ II Corinthian 4:18 HCSB

Inspiration Patch
Some people use the day to fulfill dreams while others just daydream.

Are you are dream fulfiller or a dream watcher? I refuse to let my epitaph read, "Here lies Sonie. She could have, would have or should have done great things." I do not want that for your life either. Let your life be one of achievement or accept that as long as you do nothing, expect nothing.

> **Inspiration Patch**
> *Waiting for people wastes time.*
> *If you want something, make it happen.*

If we calculated the time people spent waiting on others to help us, the hours would be immense. Unless someone shares your objective, their commitment and effort may differ considerably from yours. Be confident in your ability to make things happen. Do not give up your dreams to disapproving people.

I know people who have wasted time and missed opportunities waiting on others thus allowing them to control their destinies. Being a loner is not the answer, however time does not wait and neither should you. If you feel that waiting on someone provides some type of benefit, I hope that the benefit exceeds the value of time lost.

Some people wait because of lack of knowledge. Even if you are unfamiliar with how to do something; the answer is literally at your fingertips with the Internet. The information explains how to do things and provides a director of resources.

Do not miss opportunities. You can do whatever you set your mind to do. Believe in yourself and press forward with or without support of others.

Sonie Bigbee

Work hard and become a leader; be lazy and become a slave.

~ Proverbs 12: 24 NLT

Inspiration Patch
When you give others power, you lose control.

If you spend thousands of dollars on a new fire-engine red Lamborghini, you are not likely to toss the keys to just anyone. You've invested a lot—if not everything—into that powerful car and you want to control every aspect of it, including whom you let drive. Direct that same fervor to your life. Don't toss your life keys to anyone. Your value far exceeds that of a Lamborghini; treat yourself as such.

If you don't take control of your life, it is your fault. You are the driver in the car to your destiny. You dictate the speed, direction and interior environment as you maneuver through the obstacles on the road of life.

Inspiration Patch
Seeking recognition for a job well-done; misses opportunities to do a job well.

Get over it! Most of us want recognition for our efforts and feeling slighted is difficult. When life does not give

Patches of Inspiration™ - Harvesting Your Success

you the hurrahs you deserve, find a way to press forward. Waiting for someone to say, "Job well done," hinders your ability to grow and advance.

Activate your ability to generate intrinsic reward and know that you did a job well, even without external acknowledgement. A lack of recognition should not distract your focus.

> *But let each one examine his own work, and then he will have rejoicing in himself alone, and not in another.*
> ~ Galatians 6:4 NKJV

Inspiration Patch
If you do not celebrate your accomplishments, others won't either.

Don't minimize your accomplishments. To downplay and ignore your success undermines your progress. If you do not treat personal success as important, how can you expect others to respect the significance?

A misconception is that pride is arrogance. Accomplishments play a major role in how we influence others and build self-esteem. Achievements evoke empowerment which leads to continued growth and success. Suppressing accomplishments stunts growth.

> *Inspiration Patch*
> *If you want something, go for it!*

Initiative: proactive measures taken to get something done. Let me reiterate; if you want something, go for it. It pains me to see people waste time rather than be productive. These same people talk about what they want, but do not take the necessary steps to manifest it.

Take the initiative. Unless you are unable to move, make the effort to enhance your life. This habit is good to have on the job, off the job, young and old.

> *For each one shall bear his own load.*
> ~ Galatians 6:5 NKJV

> *Inspiration Patch*
> *Teamwork — the removal of personal motives to achieve a common goal.*

Teamwork means that you put aside your desires and motives to achieve the goal(s) of the group.

Leaders must understand that teamwork is never about personal ambitions. Team is the ability for two or more to excel above many.

T – Two or more

E – Excel

A – Above

M - Many

If this principle is a must for God, it should be a must for us.

> *Again I say to you that if two of you agree on earth concerning anything that they ask, it will be done for them by My Father in heaven, For where two or three are gathered together in My name, I am there in the midst of them.*
> ~ Matthew 18:19-20 NKJV

> *Inspiration Patch*
> *The works of others are not ladders for you.*

The climb to the top is not about who you can step on to get there. True success is about whom you lift up or bring along with you. The purpose of a ladder is to climb to another level. However, to successfully climb a ladder, it must be supported; propped against something, held by someone or have built-in reinforcements. Either way you cannot stand up a ladder without some type of support system and expect to climb it.

Consider people as support, not a wrung on a ladder upon which to step. The ladder, your mindset, is the tool to get you to the top. You have to climb the ladder yourself; others cannot do it for you. People are the support in your rise to success, without them, you cannot climb the ladder.

> *Don't be selfish; don't try to impress others. Be humble, thinking of others as better than yourselves. Don't look out only for your own interests, but take an interest in others, too.*
>
> ~ Philippians 2:3-4 NLT

In everything, therefore, treat people the same way you want them to treat you, for this is the law and the prophets.

~ Matthew 7:12 NASB

Inspiration Patch
You cannot change a person, but you can influence a person to change.

Your degree of influence may surprise you. Your personality, attitude and behaviors which reflect the core of who you are, are observed by others. Habits and personality traits are picked up from many different sources. Just as children mimic adults, adults mimic adults. For this reason, we have a subtle or covert power of influence. So, if you cannot get that person to conform, evaluate yourself and then develop new behaviors for life-changing influence.

Without wise leadership, a nation falls; there is safety in having many advisers.

~ Proverbs 11:14 NLT

Inspiration Patch
Leaders lead by example: Do as I do.

Many people want the title and "glamour" of leadership, however the responsibility is often abused as a pass to bark orders. Effective leaders do not force agendas. Their actions, behaviors and talents demonstrate leadership and guidance to others. Express your leadership like an award-winning novelist depicts a story; by showing versus telling.

Instruct the wise, and they will be even wiser. Teach the righteous, and they will learn even more.
~ Proverbs 9:9 NLT

Inspiration Patch
Power is not being on top, but the ability to put others on top.

Powerful people make things happen. What value is a title without authority? Seek opportunities that enable you to pull others along. You may not be the person at the top, but if you have a network that enables others to reach the top, that is just as powerful. A person's greatness is not measured by what they do for themselves, but what they do for others. A resourceful network and positive influence are critical to harvesting success.

Patches of Inspiration™ - Harvesting Your Success

If you think you are too important to help someone, you are only fooling yourself. You are not that important.
~ Galatians 6:3 NLT

Do not withhold good from those who deserve it when it's in your power to help them.
~ Proverbs 3:27 NLT

Inspiration Patch
Success is the ability to help others excel.

For some, success is based upon how much income we have, the title we receive or the ability to accumulate material things. True success is the ability to help others. Not many people are in a position, or willing, to help others succeed.

The ability to influence other people is powerful. You may ask, "Well, how do I influence people, if I am not a manager?" Sharing your knowledge and experiences as a mentor or coach is a direct form of influence. Indirectly, your actions can be inspirational.

Sonie Bigbee

Give and you will receive. Your gift will return to you in full—pressed down, shaken together to make room for more, running over, and poured into your lap. The amount you give will determine the amount you get back.

~ Luke 6:38 NLT

Patches of Inspiration™ - Harvesting Your Success

Create a Leadership Harvest

Seed: Something you need
- Action
- Self motivation

Root: Something you need to grow and develop
- Teamwork
- Positive influence on others
- Ability to pull others up
- Effective decision making
- Celebration of accomplishments

Weed: Something you need to remove
- Procrastination
- Negative example to others
- Laziness

Notes _____

_____

_____

_____

_____

_____

_____

_____

_____

_____

_____

Does Your Image Work?

Image is a seed and a root as it has internal and external attributes. Image is an important aspect of success and requires frequent developing. Image is more than external appearance. Perceived image, or how others see you, is often overlooked. If you amass greatness without assistance, then kudos to you. For the rest of us, a team, with a positive perception, is required.

> *Inspiration Patch*
> *Positive self image is confidence in yourself.*

Feelings drive our entire being. Think about it, if we feel good when we wake in the morning, chances are we want to look good. And if we feel like crap — you get the point. Self esteem drives confidence. Highly confident people tend to feel good and so they tend to look good.

Build your positive image. Make a conscious decision to feel good about you. Control what you can about your internal image, your thoughts and feelings.

Faith is the confidence that what we hope for will actually happen; it gives us assurance about things we cannot see.

~ Hebrews 11:1 NLT

Inspiration Patch
To walk with your head up is to believe in what you do.

Hold your head high. Even when you feel low, force yourself to stand erect with shoulders square. I guarantee that your confidence will elevate to meet your statuesque stance.

I will maintain my righteousness and never let go of it; my conscience will not reproach me as long as I live.

~ Job 27:6 NIV

Inspiration Patch
The opinions of others about you are formed by you.

How you are perceived and respected comes through the opinion of others. Now with that said, I know that opinions are formed without ever meeting or knowing a person. I also know that these same preconceived opinions can be modified upon a personal encounter. Ultimately, the opinion is formed by YOU.

> *Pray for us, for we are sure that we have a good conscience, desiring to conduct ourselves honorably in all things.*
> ~ Hebrews 13:18 NASB

Inspiration Patch
A smile transfers your joy.

A smile is powerful because it symbolizes happiness, peace and joy. My mother referred to people who never smiled as "sour apples." Enjoy life. Bundle yourself with a smile like an overcoat during an Alaskan winter; deflect the cold and have a warm, fuzzy feeling inside.

Inspiration Patch
Do not lose yourself in anything you do. If you cannot find what you are, others do not know who you are.

Identity. You have been gifted and blessed with your greatness: uniqueness. We forget the strength of being one of a kind and lose ourselves emulating others. Know who you are, be who you are and require others to do the same.

> *Inspiration Patch*
> *Originality is self discovery without influence.*

Webster's Dictionary describes originality as new and unusual. I view originality as different and different is okay! Companies scramble for talent to create the next new and original idea. Let your gifts flow. Use them to discover and be who you are without influence. Influence can be internal — the quiet voice that fills our minds with thoughts of self worth — and imputed by outside factors like environment and people.

When you know who you are and your purpose, you find peace and contentment. Permitting influences to invade during the discovery phase stirs up confusion and stalls progress. Your mission is to find your original blueprint; your purpose.

> *Inspiration Patch*
> *If you allow others to validate you, then you do not know who you are.*

Have you ever been at a point of validation where you waited for others to affirm or reject your idea? To make matters worse, depending upon the feedback, your mood shifted from jubilation to melancholy. Self confidence will withstand the opinions of naysayers, so don't give up your power.

I once worked at a company that I felt did not acknowledge my contributions. Influenced by lack of recognition and mistreatment, I allowed my feelings to consume me and it eventually affected my performance. When I realized that I didn't need them to give me a certificate or a pat on the back, my frustration subsided. I knew that I had a lot to offer and when the situation became too annoying, I made a change. I flourished in an environment that otherwise could have been my downfall.

> *Do you see a man skilled in his work? He will stand in the presence of kings. He will not stand in the presence of unknown men.*
> ~ Proverbs 22:29 HCSB

Inspiration Patch
If no one is listening, stop talking. People tune in to hear a soft voice and tune out when a loud mouth speaks.

Patches of Inspiration™ - Harvesting Your Success

No one wants the negative connotations of the loud-mouth label; always talking and never listening. Immense knowledge comes from listening and observing. The best leaders are great listeners. A facilitation technique to redirect attention from a side conversation back to the presenter is silence. The nonverbal interaction draws attention to the extracurricular conversation and puts the offenders on the spot.

Inspiration Patch
If you settle on yourself, others will settle on you, too.

To settle, or give up, is to relinquish peace of mind. The beauty is that most everything is up to you because settlement is a choice, not a requirement.

Your objective is to go as far as possible. This drive separates the people who have what they want from those who do not. Would you agree that living life in the "I'm okay" or "I'm barely making it" lane is frustrating? Why put yourself through such monotony, when so much opportunity is available with focus and effort?

> *Inspiration Patch*
> *A true test of character is how a person responds in difficult times.*

Character is pertinent to your image. It emerges as turbulence swells the sea of life. The storms will come and go. Don't let your character bounce with the ebb and flow only to be washed ashore tattered and worn. Hold firm to your life jacket of character and image. You may be battered and bruised but your character will be in tact. You can walk the sandy beaches without regret or fear consequences.

Do not deceive or cheat one another.
~ Leviticus 19:11 NLT

Providing honorable things, not only in the sight of the Lord, but also in the sight of men.
~ II Corinthian 8:21 NKJV

Patches of Inspiration™ - Harvesting Your Success

Create an Image Harvest

Seed: Something you need
- Positive image
- High self esteem
- Belief in self
- Spirit of joy
- Originality
- Validation of self
- Good character

Root: Something you need to grow and develop
- Loving self
- Daily joy
- Self discovery
- Good listening skills

Weed: Something you need to remove
- Negative image
- Low self esteem
- Validation from others
- Loud mouth
- Settling on self

Notes _____

_____

_____

_____

_____

_____

The Meaningful Network and Environment

The network patch is a seed and root. Building a meaningful network is dependent upon the right environment; one conducive to learning. If you are the smartest person in the group, expand your circle of friends. A strong network has residual benefits, opens doors and expands opportunities. You want to know people who can help you achieve goals.

When my father ran for office with the local school board, the first thing he did was find key people to support his campaign. He knew that a strong network would increase his chances to win the election. Thanks to his early effort to develop a strong team, he won.

Research has proven that we are products of our environment. That being the case, create an atmosphere that produces the product or results you desire.

Inspiration Patch
Living without family is living without life.

What is life? Experience. Vibrancy. Joy. Meaning. Don't become so consumed with living that you forget to share your life with others including those beyond biological lineage. Family is the people who support and encourage you to enjoy a life of abundance. Success is great; success with family is greater.

> *This is My commandment, that you love one another as I have loved you. Greater love has no one than this, than to lay down one's life for his friends.*
> ~ John 15:12-13 NKJV

Inspiration Patch
A parent symbolizes life's triumphant stand.

A parent—with or without blood ties—can rear a child. The absence of a parent is a common excuse for lack of success. Don't let this void lead to a life of hatred, resentment and frustration because the mindset impairs growth. Anyone or anything that teaches positive lessons on how to win, grow and make a stand can be a surrogate parent.

> *Inspiration Patch*
> *The things closest to you should be a source of joy and peace.*

People introduce chaos and misery into their lives because they have surrounded themselves with a disorganized way of living. Your mind, body and spirit are fed by the things that are in and around you. Statistically, individuals who are in negative environments and with negative people, tend to be negative. Guard the people and energy you let into your inner circle. Whomever you let close to you should bring positive energy, joy and peace.

Make every effort to keep yourselves united in the Spirit, binding yourselves together with peace.
~ Ephesians 4:3 NLT

> *Inspiration Patch*
> *Remember the root of your seed; how you are planted is how you will grow.*

The pace of anything is achieved at the beginning of its existence. With respect to crops, the seed, soil, fertilizer and water affect the outcome of the plant. If the seed is not properly planted and maintained, the end result could be disastrous to the crop. How much money would farmers lose if they did not take the planting process serious? Like the farmer committed to toiling his fields, take cautionary steps to ensure a flourishing horn of plenty. Plant seeds of purpose. Utilize resources that will optimize your yield. You want your life to be a harvest of purposeful growth, not a famine plagued with infestation and disease.

> *The seeds of good deeds become a tree of life; a wise person wins friends.*
> ~ Proverbs 11:30 NLT

> *Now he who plants and he who waters are one, and each one will receive his own reward according to his own labor.*
> ~ I Corinthians 3:8 NKJV

Inspiration Patch
Build relationships with people who can elevate you. Build friendships with people who make you happy.

Relationship building is critical to your success. Too many people waste time with the wrong people; those who do not nurture your growth. As the saying goes, "It is not what you know, but who you know."

Look at relationships as building blocks of opportunity with people who can elevate you spiritually, mentally and physically. Friendships exist with individuals who share a winning common purpose. Friendships can fall short of encouraging growth and development. Relationships, on the other hand, are deeply rooted friendships that involve a great deal of feeling. If you are going to move people from the friendship to the relationship category, make sure that they are a building block worthy of your feelings.

> *Don't befriend angry people or associate with hot-tempered people, or you will learn to be like them and endanger your soul.*
> ~ Proverbs 22:24-25 NLT

> *Finally, all of you, live in harmony with one another; be sympathetic, love as brothers, be compassionate and humble.*
> ~ I Peter 3:8 NIV

Inspiration Patch
Enlarge your territory, you can have it all.

Think big! Cliché, but it is true. The bigger you think, the larger you grow. Don't box yourself in with your thoughts and ambitions. I encourage you to go outside of the box that marks the boundaries of your life. I was surprised to learn that many people never travel more than fifteen miles from home. They have a limited perspective on what life has to offer. Doubling their territory to a thirty-mile radius could have a tremendous expansion into their lives. Expand your perimeter. Enlarge your territory. Venture beyond your immediate neighborhood and check out the world. The larger your territory, the more you can achieve.

Create a Network Harvest

Seed: Something you need
- People of meaning
- Symbolic figure of growth
- Positive people
- Building relationships

Root: Something you need to grow and develop
- Meaningful relationships
- Expanded territory

Weed: Something you need to remove
- Negative people
- People that do not build you
- People that cannot help you grow

Notes _____
_____
_____
_____
_____
_____
_____
_____
_____
_____
_____
_____

Courage to Maneuver Obstacles and Challenges

Courage is a seed and root that enables you to move past your fears of the unknown. The lack of courage decreases your risk-taking factor; a significant component to success.

Many successful people have addressed the sneers and banter of doubters. Accused of being crazy for pursuing their dreams, they persisted. Despite the propensity to fail, they remained in pursuit. Use their actions as an example; get over your fears, develop the faith like Jesus and walk on water.

Inspiration Patch
Face a challenge as a mountain and it seems hard to climb.
Face a challenge as a goal and it becomes achievable.

I venture to say that a high percentage of people have not climbed a mountain. Maybe the exhilaration at the peak is minimized by the challenges on the slope. Possibly the fear factor masks the adventurous thrill. Whatever the reason, few choose to endure a task that seems overwhelming.

A great level of fulfillment is gained by achieving a goal. Your perception of a challenge can make it a seemingly impossible task or an achievable goal. What vantage point will you take? Although either perspective requires work to manifest, a challenge seems to be exponential in difficulty when compared to a goal.

Be creative. Determine your overall objective, dissect it into manageable goals and then focus on the reward.

> *I tell you the truth, you can say to this mountain, "May you be lifted up and thrown into the sea," and it will happen. But you must really believe it will happen and have no doubt in your heart. I tell you, you can pray for anything, and if you believe that you've received it, it will be yours.*
> ~ Mark 11:23-24 NLT

Inspiration Patch
Climbing life's ladder is like climbing a mountain.
You may get bumps and bruises on the long, uphill journey, but at the top, the view is spectacular.

Patches of Inspiration™ - Harvesting Your Success

Most people want to enjoy the pleasures at the top, but few are willing to enlist the responsibility and effort to get there. Challenges and obstacles will come that will make you want to give up. During these times, pull on the strength within and tell yourself that you are going to make it. Instead of dwelling on where you are or the task you have to take on, focus on the reward. The view from the top is spectacular.

> *You will go out in joy and be led forth in peace; the mountains and hills will burst into song before you, and all the trees of the field will clap their hands.*
> ~ Isaiah 55:12 NIV

Inspiration Patch
Obstacles are tools of creativity.

Obstacles are those nasty little things that impede goal achievement and can ultimately PREVENT success, if they are not effectively handled.

Instead of viewing obstacles as hindrances, find a way to work around or plow through them — tools of creativity.

Let's say for example, you have decided to go back to college to reinvent yourself and change vocations. Two obstacles stand in your way:

1. You have a full time job.
2. You have a family that needs your time.

A traditional back-to-school plan probably will not work for you. Does that mean you give up on that goal? Absolutely not! Many colleges offer accelerated learning, evening classes and online courses to accommodate the demands of non-traditional students. Contact the Admissions Office and start materializing your goal.

For the Lord is your security. He will keep your foot from being caught in a trap.
~ Proverbs 3:26 NLT

For I can do everything through Christ, who gives me strength.
~ Philippians 4:13 NLT

Inspiration Patch
Change your circumstance and it becomes your past; otherwise it dictates your future.

Webster's Dictionary defines a circumstance as a condition or fact that must be considered in determining a course of action. "Course of action." Too many people use their circumstances like an airplane pilot uses a holding pattern: move in circles until the situation works itself out. Don't give up your power to circumstance. When God directs you to land, redirect the airplane to your course destination.

My daughter wants to be a fashion designer, however living in the good old Midwest may complicate the launch of her career. If she decides to terminate the endeavor because residing in Ohio prevented her from achieving that goal, I will inform her that she is making excuses. The right course of action might be to relocate to a city more conducive to advancement in her field of choice. She could appropriately guide her future by assessing the potential hurdles and determine an appropriate course of action.

Success Formula for Change

Situation Recognition + Course of Action = Change

> *Yet what we suffer now is nothing compared to the glory He will reveal to us later.*
> ~ Romans 8:18 NLT

> *Inspiration Patch*
> *Tumultuous situations need immediate attention.*

When turmoil enters the picture, all is not lost. Address turmoil head on because left unattended, the situation can explode like fuel thrown on an open flame. Your objective is to put out the flame. You may find that things were not as bad as you thought. In the event of relevant turmoil, take time to address the issue(s) and create a course of action.

> *Let your gentleness be known to all men. The Lord is at hand.*
> ~ Philippians 4:5 NKJV

> *Inspiration Patch*
> *Courage is acting on your fears.*

Fear paralysis is a handicap. Propelling forward despite your fears, demonstrates courage. You are stating that no matter what handicap exists; I am still moving forward in a way that says I can do it.

Patches of Inspiration™ - Harvesting Your Success

This is My command—be strong and courageous! Do not be afraid or discouraged. For the Lord your God is with you wherever you go.

~ Joshua 1:9 NLT

Inspiration Patch
Courage transforms fear into pursuit.

Courage starts as a mind game. To overcome paralyzing fear, tell yourself that you are not afraid. Even if you aren't totally convinced, move forward into a state of pursuit.

Inspiration Patch
Freedom removes bondage and captivity.

People around the world give their lives in search of freedom. The ability to do whatever you want, whenever you want is liberating.

Even with limitless opportunities, we miss the freedom train by attaching unnecessary strings: bondage and captivity. Life brings sufficient issues, so why intensify the inevitable? The more free you are, the more you can do.

For you have been called to live in freedom, my brothers and sisters. But don't use your freedom to satisfy your sinful nature. Instead, use your freedom to serve one another in love.

~ Galatians 5:13 NLT

Inspiration Patch
If a situation holds you captive, break free!

Many people live in bondage; mental, physical, spiritual and financial bondage. No matter what form it takes, bondage, or imprisonment, of any kind is not good as it prevents growth and hinders success. Identify your captor, name it "freedom" and break free! If removal from bondage is your will, you will find a way.

For you have been called to live in freedom, my brothers and sisters. But don't use your freedom to satisfy your sinful nature. Instead, use your freedom to serve one another in love.

~ Galatians 5:13 NLT

Patches of Inspiration™ - Harvesting Your Success

Create a Courage Harvest

Seed: Something you need
- Courage
- Freedom
- Movement

Root: Something you need to grow and develop
- Ability to face challenges
- Ability to change circumstances
- Pursuit
- Progress

Weed: Something you need to remove
- Bad circumstances
- Turmoil
- Fear
- Handicaps
- Obstacles
- Bondage and captivity

Notes _____

_____

_____

_____

_____

_____

_____

_____

_____

State of Mind

Science has proven that state of mind influences every aspect of a person's life. Simply put, with the right thoughts, you can get the right results. Guard your thoughts daily and dismiss anything that is contrary.

> *Inspiration Patch*
> *Thinking paints the picture of life. Let your canvas be positive thoughts bring life while negative thoughts create death.*

Life or death through your thoughts can be both figurative and literal. Negative thoughts paralyze. Consider a man who has been in good physical health. Following a routine check up, he learns that he has terminal cancer. He can internalize the news and wait for death or he can dwell on the promises of God and command his healing to manifest. How much impact does the power of positive thinking have on cancer survival?

When the medical community determines a patient to be brain dead, irreversible loss of brain function has occurred.

Although the heart may continue to beat, assisted by a ventilator, the patient is diagnosed as dead with no hope for recovery. To put it bluntly, it is time to pull the plug. Keep your mind alive and well with thoughts of encouragement, inspiration and hope.

> *Do not conform any longer to the pattern of this world, but be transformed by the renewing of your mind. Then you will be able to test and approve what God's will is—His good, pleasing and perfect will.*
>
> ~ Romans 12:2 NIV

Inspiration Patch
Own your mind, it owns you.

Success is yours and when perceived reality — we don't know what's working behind the scenes on our behalf — says otherwise, change your thinking immediately. We rationalize ourselves out of glory by thinking our vision is impossible or crazy.

Although many people desire to write and publish a book, few see the dream to fruition. The industry can be complicated and costly for a novice. So when the urge to publish ignited within me, doubt came along for the ride. "It will never happen. You don't know anything about publishing." Instead of staying in the boat, I opted to be a water walker. I researched the industry and dove into every website, article and publication I could find on writing and publishing. I spoke with numerous industry experts. I could have rationalized myself out of pursuing a life goal, but I dismissed the doubtful thoughts. And since you are reading *Patches of Inspiration*, I can check "write and publish a book" off of my to-do list.

> *What do you mean, 'If I can,' Jesus asked. Anything is possible if a person believes.*
> ~ Mark 9:23 NLT

Inspiration Patch
The state of your mind is a joy locator.

Joy is generated internally. External influences may affect your happiness, but not the joy that resides deep within you. If joy was found in possessions and people, then the wealthy would not be plagued with drug addiction and suicide. The rich and famous are known to travel the world, enjoy lavish lifestyles and want for nothing, yet they still experience a great deal of misery. Why? Because they do not realize that true joy is a state of mind.

> *Inspiration Patch*
> *If you cannot find peace, create it!*

Peace and internal turmoil cannot co-exist. If you cannot find peace in your life, create it. Carve out a weekly time slot in which you let everyone know that you do not want to be disturbed. Even if it's ten minutes, be consistent about your quiet time. Take a walk, listen to your favorite song or read. Whatever healthy means you use to refresh and rejuvenate pursue it.

> *Depart from evil, and do good; seek peace, and pursue it.*
> ~ Psalm 34:14

> *Inspiration Patch*
> *Mediation is a time to reflect on life's direction.*

I remind myself to take my own advice on this patch. Meditation, or time out when applied to disciplining children, not only helps you slow down; the quiet time frees you to have creative thoughts. The direction of your life is not something to take lightly. To make adequate life plans, spend more time in thought and preparation than execution.

> *Study this book of instruction continually. Meditate on it day and night so you will be sure to obey everything written in it. Only then will you prosper and succeed in all you do.*
> ~ Joshua 1:8 NLT

Inspiration Patch
Misery is not an option, happiness is.

Omit misery from your vocabulary. Strive for daily happiness and don't let anything or anyone take it away. Your mindset and level of happiness drives your ambition, actions and success. Sour apples, as my mother labeled them, choose to be mean, miserable and depressed. With a little effort to find happiness, the negative energy could be redirected to productivity. Make happiness a daily mission and an expectation for you and those around you.

Inspiration Patch
Put yourself in a trance. If you bring your dreams to you, they will come true.

As a child, I would lay on the floor by my father's speakers. I listened to music and daydreamed about driving a convertible and standing on stage speaking to hundreds of people. As an adult, I still find myself daydreaming because it projects me to a place I desire. It creates a vision that ignites a passion of pursuit. Daydreaming is a motivator that makes dreams real. Take yourself to a place where you can image and even see yourself living your dreams. In the 1989 movie, *Field of Dreams*, the great line, "If you build it, they will come," resounded the need to go from dream making to reality achieving.

Inspiration Patch
Fill up on things that nourish your life.

Nourishment provides our bodies with essential elements for good health and optimal performance. Nourishment is not just about the food we ingest, it also involves the mind and spirit.

> *Getting wisdom is the wisest thing you can do! And whatever else you do, develop good judgment.*
> ~ Proverbs 4:7 NLT

> *A house is built by wisdom and becomes strong through good sense. Through knowledge its rooms are filled with all sorts of precious riches and valuables.*
> ~ Proverbs 24:3-4 NLT

Inspiration Patch
Your situation is temporary. Forget the things that do not matter and rejoice in the things that do.

Too many of us harp on the today. Today is just that, today. Lord willing, you will have tomorrow. Instead of dwelling on your right-now situation and meaningless things, find joy and understanding in what really matters.

> *Furthermore, because we are united with Christ, we have received an inheritance from God, for He chose us in advance, and He makes everything work out according to His plan.*
> ~ Ephesians 1:11 NLT

Patches of Inspiration™ - Harvesting Your Success

Create a State of Mind Harvest

Seed: Something you need
- Positive thoughts
- Joy
- Peace
- Happiness

Root: Something you need to grow and develop
- Mental nourishment
- Mental guide
- Rationalization
- Meditation
- Daydreaming

Weed: Something you need to remove
- Negative thoughts
- Misery

Notes _____

_____
_____
_____
_____
_____
_____
_____
_____
_____

Owning Goals, Understanding Opportunity

Like perennials grow year after year goals should be perpetual seeds. Goal setting and opportunities are essential to success. Learn how to recognize and act on opportunity while setting goals and taking action to achieve them.

> *Inspiration Patch*
> *Own the opportunities presented to you. If you do not take advantage of them, someone else will.*

Every time you miss an opportunity, someone else seizes the moment. Smart people look for opportunities, some of which come knocking at the proverbial front door.

After speaking at a community event, I was approached about hosting a thirty-minute motivational radio talk show. I was also asked if I had a book. I had tossed around the idea of writing a book and had even carved out some concepts, but nothing was complete. The conversations around the talk show led to an offer of guidance and free promotion for my book. To ensure that I could take full advantage of this potential opportunity, I worked tirelessly to finish my book and website. My family and I relocated so the talk show conversations stalled however, the book is tangible.

Don't be afraid of opportunities, act on them. They may not come around again. The opportunity you disregard could be the one to change your life.

Therefore, whenever we have the opportunity, we should do good to everyone—especially to those in the family of faith.
~ Galatians 6:10 NLT

Inspiration Patch
Look around you to find life's open doors. It is through these doors that opportunities are found.

"When one door closes, another one opens." You've probably heard that statement in a myriad of forms, but the root is the same: look for the entry way to whatever it is that you want to achieve. Many business leaders started at the bottom of the company. The careers of many A-list actors began with small roles. The entry way, albeit modest, led to high-paying, high-profile positions. Ascension happens over a period of time. Identify the mountaintop you want to stand on, find the entry way and climb.

> *We must quickly carry out the tasks assigned us by the one who sent us. The night is coming, and then no one can work.*
>
> ~ John 9:4 NLT

Inspiration Patch
The eyes of tomorrow's opportunities are watching you today.

You never know the origin of your next opportunity. Know that someone is observing you and using those observations to shape their perception of you.

I hesitate when someone asks me for a business favor and they have not presented themselves in a professional manner. Although we may have a cordial, friendly relationship, professional recommendation takes on a different dynamic. Character, a snap shot of a person's moral and ethical fiber, is important when making professional recommendations. Endorsement is transference of credibility therefore the likelihood that others will associate the character of the two parties is highly probable.

Statistics indicate that upon landing that dream job, future promotions are based 85% on relationships and 15%

skill. The numbers confirm that in business, it's not what you know, but who you know.

Present yourself in such a manner that someone would be willing to endorse you. The talk show opportunity came when the general manager (GM) observed my presentation skills and demeanor. The connection came through a community event, but the endorsement came through a sorority sister who knew the GM. She affirmed me and validated my character. Since people watch your character, present yourself well to avoid missing opportunities.

For we are each responsible for our own conduct.
~ Galatians 6:5 NLT

Inspiration Patch
Opportunities are equal. Desire and success are not.

It has always been my motto that everyone enters the playing field at the same time in life. For the most part, most of us have a fair chance to educate ourselves and pursue opportunities. It is sort of like going back to kindergarten. All the children are somewhere around the age of five or six, energetic and full of promise. Unfortunately, when you fast-forward that same group of children twelve years, many times the energy and promise dwindle or are completely lost.

With opportunity being an even playing field, do not allow lack of care or desire hinder you from success. See life as an even playing field. You must desire to be successful. Find opportunities in life that allow you to do just that.

For some of you, you may be saying what if life threw me a curve ball. What if I had or am taking care of myself. What if I have or am living in a disadvantaged situation. My response to you would be that there are resources all around you to help you be successful. You must find and use the necessary resources that apply to your situation coupled with the desire built in you to be successful. It is possible!

When I was a single mother on public assistance and living in subsidized housing, I technically was in a disadvantaged situation. I sought out and used the resources available to me along with my desire to rise up from that situation and still achieve my goals.

> *Lazy people want much but get little, but those who work hard will prosper.*
>
> ~ Proverbs 13:4 NLT

> *Inspiration Patch*
> *If you want new opportunities, pursue them.*

Have you ever said, "I need a change" or "I want something different"? In essence, you want a new opportunity. Some opportunities are right in front of us but we have to dig for others. Either way, nothing happens without action. Proactive or reactive, do something.

> *Inspiration Patch*
> *Goals without action are dreams deferred.*

Faith without work is dead and goals without action are lost dreams. Many people talk about their desires without realizing that by putting action behind the passion goals can be achieved.

Have you ever met a dreamer? A dreamer loves to talk about what he or she is going to do one day. Start a business, travel the world, become an actor. The aspirations consume the conversation and upon your next encounter, they have either migrated to a new dream or still hanging onto the old ones. No action, just talk.

Transform your desires into goals with action by developing a detailed plan. For example, if your goal is to own a business, research the industry: competition, customer demographics, profit margin, start-up costs. Meet with business owners, confer with the local Small Business Association, take college classes. Just do it.

> *Now that you know these things, you will be blessed if you do them.*
> ~ John 13:17 NIV

Inspiration Patch
Build a strategy, design a smart plan, achieve a goal.

Achieving a goal can be as easy or as complex as you make it. Work smart with a step-by-step playbook that captures your strategy. Approach goal achieving like a road trip and consider the following:

- Where are you going?
- When do you want to arrive?
- What method will you use to get there?
- How long it will take to get there?
- Where are you going to stay?
- How much will it cost?
- What do you need to pack?

Patches of Inspiration™ - Harvesting Your Success

Okay, you get my point. A ton of steps are needed to ensure that you have a safe and rewarding travel experience. Apply this strategic plan to your life by answering the following:

- Where do I want to be?
- How much time am I allocating to achieve that goal?
- What will it take to get there (education, training, resources, networking)?
- How committed am I to getting there?
- What is my risk and reward?
- How am I going to make it happen?

A clear life plan, much like a business plan, outlines where you want to go and how to get there. As the saying goes, "Fail to plan and you plan to fail."

Good planning and hard work lead to prosperity, but hasty shortcuts lead to poverty.
~ Proverbs 21:5 NLT

Plans go wrong for lack of advice; many advisers bring success.
~ Proverbs 15:22 NLT

> **Inspiration Patch**
> *Goals are cyclical; as one is achieved, another is created.*

If we applied this cyclical concept to the goal of opening a business, once established, the next goal may be to expand into new markets or increase product offerings.

We live in a world of change: jobs, technology, science, medicine and government change constantly. Whether out of necessity or innovation, change is inevitable. Stay ahead of progress, and like a game of chess, plan your next move. Checkmate!

> **Inspiration Patch**
> *The contentment necessary to enjoy life can also stagnate it. Don't let complacency stunt your growth.*

Contentment can appear soon after a goal is achieved and halt forward progress. If nothing else in your life is consistent, growth—spiritual, educational, financial and personal—should be.

When an interviewer asked, "How much is enough," John D. Rockefeller replied, "Just a little more." The drive and fortitude of successful people amazes me. These multi-millionaires are not content with the wealth they've amassed and their cogs of ingenuity are in perpetual

Patches of Inspiration™ - Harvesting Your Success

motion. So as you grow, be thankful for what you have and optimistic about what is to come.

> *Not that I was ever in need, for I have learned how to be content with whatever I have.*
> ~ Philippians 4:11 NLT

Create an Opportunity Harvest

Seed: Something you need
- Goals
- Positive image
- Desire
- Action

Root: Something you need to grow and develop
- Opportunity
- Open doors
- Relationships
- Strategy

Weed: Something you need to remove
- Fear
- Negative image
- Laziness
- Contentment

Notes _____
_____
_____
_____
_____
_____
_____
_____

Align Your Pursuit with Your Priorities

The root of pursuit is capitalizing on opportunities created or presented.

Learn to keep things in perspective. Start by fully understanding your priorities and then align your pursuits accordingly.

Inspiration Patch
Chase the irreplaceable.

Many people waste time chasing the wrong dreams. As a society, we put too much emphasis on what we have and what we can get. During my tenure in Corporate America, I saw families destroyed while chasing the high-paying jobs and big offices. Why? To buy big things. These same people soon found that their loyalty to the company was not reciprocated and they were left with materialistic possessions and big bills.

Be motivated to acquire those things that have meaning and value. Material possessions depreciate in value, yet have 100% replacement potential. Memories, time and people are irreplaceable. Be mindful of true versus perceived value.

> *Don't wear yourself out trying to get rich. Be wise enough to know when to quit.*
> ~ Proverbs 23:4 NLT

> *Don't love money; be satisfied with what you have. For God has said, "I will never fail you. I will never abandon you."*
> ~ Hebrews 13:5 NLT

Yet true godliness with contentment is itself great wealth. After all, we brought nothing with us when we came into the world, and we can't take anything with us when we leave it. So if we have enough food and clothing, let us be content.
~ I Timothy 6:6-8 NLT

Inspiration Patch
Seek the things that matter most. Selfish gain is time spent in vain.

Patches of Inspiration™ - Harvesting Your Success

Chase things of purpose and meaning for others and display the special gifts you bring to the world. While working to be a blessing to others, you'll find personal reward.

> *If you help the poor, you are lending to the Lord—and He will repay you!*
> ~ Proverbs 19:17 NLT

> *Trust in your money and down you go! But the godly flourish like leaves in spring.*
> ~ Proverbs 11:28 NLT

Inspiration Patch
Seek wholeness. Missing pieces lead to incompleteness.

Have you ever assembled a bicycle or piece of furniture? You spent hours following the instructions to the final detail only to end up with extra parts. Now I'm not talking about spare parts provided by the manufacturer. I mean parts that should have been included in the assembly process but were some how over looked. It's cause for alarm especially if you plan to put your child on that potential defective and hazardous bicycle.

Inefficient operation occurs with missing parts. Before a doctor goes into surgery, a checklist is used to verify that the instruments are in place and functioning properly. Imagine what would happen if the checklist was not verified and during surgery a necessary instrument was not present. Disastrous.

> *Inspiration Patch*
> *Until you know there is nothing left for you to do, you have work to do.*

Giving up too soon can be just as detrimental as never starting. Just because things are going well, does not mean that you settle into a status-quo lifestyle. We have been blessed with so many gifts and talents that lay dormant because life's daily rigors trivialized or minimized their worth.

Maybe you have something inside of you leading you to participate in an organization. Your talents would be a great asset but you choose not to participate. Tap into your talent and complete works.

Do not let your talents and abilities sit on a shelf inside of you. Use your talents to the fullest of your ability until you know with all certainty that you have done all you can do.

God has given each of you a gift from His great variety of spiritual gifts. Use them well to serve one another.

~ I Peter 4:10 NLT

Inspiration Patch
Works without passion are works without meaning.

Passion puts meaning and feeling into actions. Whatever you do, make sure that it is something that you have strong feelings towards; either love or hate. If you hate something with enough passion, it may be your purpose to change it. Passion combined with effort brings joy, happiness and often times peace.

Inspiration Patch
If you hope for something, you desire to see it manifest.

Hope is another way of saying desire. Desire coincides with drive towards a mission or goal. The things we hope for have to go from being a dream in our head to pursuit of purpose.

Desire is the driving force to make things happen. In the *Patches of Inspiration™ Success Model* (see page 134), desire is the second element. Once you identify a goal, you need desire to go after it. If desire is not a variable in the equation, purpose and drive are moot.

> *But if you remain in me and my words remain in you, you may ask for anything you want, and it will be granted!*
> ~ John 15:7 NLT

Inspiration Patch
Life is a bicycle; the more you peddle, the further you go.

Unless you hop on a stationary bicycle, the objective for peddling is to go somewhere. Your motivation to ride may be leisure, competition or exercise, but the purpose is to move to a new destination. So if you are not in your retirement years, enjoying everyday as it comes, keep your momentum. When you hop on your bicycle of life, you should be going somewhere.

Fast-forward your life movie five years. Will you be in a different place? A place of more education, wealth or a better career. Hopefully, in that timeframe some aspect of your life is further along.

Patches of Inspiration™ - Harvesting Your Success

If you've attended a high school or college class reunion, you can attest to the variation in success. Some classmates have excelled beyond the "most likely to succeed" superlatives, while others lived up to the moniker of class clown.

Set the purpose of your life's ride. Peddle fast and far, so when you take a water break and look back, you can see how far you've traveled.

> *Inspiration Patch*
> *Let the desires of your heart motivate you to fulfill your aspirations and dreams.*

Burning desires ignite the passion, however dream fulfillment is your responsibility. If your desire is to become a corporate executive, then let that motivate your daily activities. Networking with executives and their secretaries will expand your knowledge. No one is going to force you to fulfill your dreams. Only you can make that happen!

> *Inspiration Patch*
> *A mission is an uninterrupted path to victory.*

To be on a mission means that you are not going to stop until you achieve what you set out to do. During a military reconnaissance mission, troops advance into the enemy's camp. Retreating is not an option until "mission accomplished" echoes through the two-way radio.

During your quest for victory, when obstacles and failures arise, look for creative ways to press forward. Fight the good fight of faith and claim your spoils of war.

> *Inspiration Patch*
> *Be relentless in the pursuit of your dreams; they were meant for you.*

You will be blessed with people and opportunities that will help you achieve your dreams. However, at the end of the day, the responsibility is yours. Just like a marathon runner does not stop until crossing the finish line, be relentless in your pursuit. Your dreams are meant for you, so they are up to you to fulfill. Don't be the person that lets you down.

Patches of Inspiration™ - Harvesting Your Success

Create a Pursuit Harvest

Seed: Something you need
- Action
- Inspiration
- Drive
- Purpose
- Passion

Root: Something you need to grow and develop
- Alignment
- Passion

Weed: Something you need to remove
- Chasing the wrong things
- Incompleteness
- Selfish gain
- Dead works

Notes _____

_____
_____
_____
_____
_____
_____
_____
_____
_____

Failure is Not So Bad

Failure, a normal part of life, is a weed to minimize and remove. Do not fear failure because it provides lessons and success is contingent upon learning how to manage it. The key to succeeding through failure is to recognize when it is taking place, develop a plan and change course quickly.

Inspiration Patch
Common sense prevents acts of stupidity.

We do not give enough credit to plain old common sense—a gift that draws on instinct for a well-rounded perspective. It is the innate understanding and guide to living.

> *People ruin their lives by their own foolishness and then are angry at the Lord.*
> ~ Proverbs 19:3 NLT

> *Inspiration Patch*
> *Life is not hard, mistakes are.*

People put too much emphasis on life being hard or even complicated. Is it life that is complicated or involvement in situations and relationships that complicate life?

Life is about making good choices, maximizing opportunity and minimizing mistakes, otherwise the result could be adverse consequences. Mistakes are expected, however, recovery takes time and effort. If your focus is on mistake recovery, progress is secondary.

How do you minimize mistakes?

1. Surround yourself with smart people
2. Make wise decisions on factual information
3. Be a consistent planner
4. Have a backup plan
5. Know when to change course

Early identification of a mistake is critical. The sooner the indiscretion is noted, the sooner correction can begin. Recognizing the time and need to change course could be the difference between a smooth or rocky recovery.

Sonie Bigbee

People who accept discipline are on the pathway to life, but those who ignore correction will go astray.

~ Proverbs 10:17 NLT

Inspiration Patch
Failures are a platform for tomorrow's success.

Failure is deemed unsuccessful, unreliable, faulty and a number of other negative words. However during life's failures we learn the most. The lessons are invaluable because they cannot be bought and no book can teach them.

In the event of failure, assess the shortfall and commit to doing things different the next time. Position yourself to avoid potential pitfalls and use failures as a platform to success the next go around.

A failed experience should not discourage or turn you off from moving forward. Let the failures energize you with more knowledge and a smarter game plan.

When I co-owned my sports team, my business partner and I were unable to secure investor capital to sustain the franchise. After an enormous amount of effort, we made the decision to fold the team. Many people saw that as a failure. For me, it was an unprecedented learning experience. The knowledge gave me a new layer of

Patches of Inspiration™ - Harvesting Your Success

professional maturity that benefits me today. I appreciate the technically "failed" opportunity because without it, I may not have identified the platform that enabled me to rise higher.

> *You therefore must endure hardship as a good soldier of Jesus Christ.*
> ~ II Timothy 2:3 NKJV

Inspiration Patch
When you see that you are falling, grab a rope and pull yourself up.

When we fall the only thing left to do is rise, however the longer the drop, the more difficult the upward climb. Don't wait until you bottom out to find a solution. During your fall, look for an escape route. Early identification of your solution is motivation to get back on your way.

Sonie Bigbee

The list below contains possible solutions for life events:

Event	Possible Solution
Divorce	Marriage counseling
Bankruptcy	Financial counseling
Business Closing	Small business consultant
Poor Grades	Tutor

Rejoice in our confident hope. Be patient in trouble, and keep on praying.
~ Romans 12:12 NLT

Inspiration Patch
Seasons are temporary.

Seasons come and go. You can determine how long each season lasts. If you do not like what is taking place in your life, make a change. Just as seasons vary in temperature and beauty; your life will vary in complexity, happiness and meaning. Take each season as a memory in the making and make the most of it.

Patches of Inspiration™ - Harvesting Your Success

Teaching them to observe everything I have commanded you. And remember, I am with you always, to the end of the age.

~ Matthew 28:20 HCSB

I can do all things through Christ which strengtheneth me.

~ Philippians 4:13 KJV

Success is yours. Any goals that you set, you can achieve. Success is real and through an organic process of seeding, rooting and weeding, it can happen for you.

Create a Failure Harvest

Seed: Something you need
- Common sense
- Wisdom
- Support
- Solutions

Root: Something you need to grow and develop
- Instinct
- Smart network
- Back up plan
- Ability to rise

Weed: Something you need to remove
- Complications
- Bad path

Notes _____

_____

_____

_____

_____

_____

_____

_____

_____

_____

_____

Patches of Inspiration™
Harvest Study Guide

The purpose of this study guide is to reflect on the reading material while making a personal connection between yourself and Patches of Inspiration.

Make a Spiritual Connection

Filling Your Core

Think about the things in life that fill the core of your inner person. List them in order of priority and time spent.

_____
_____
_____

If God was not number one on the list, what can do to make Him first in your daily living? List some daily activities you can do to fill your life with more of God and less of everything else.

_____
_____
_____

Asking God

The first step to getting what we want from God is to ASK. Think of three things you want to ask God for and list them below.

Prayer Request #1

_____
_____
_____

Prayer Request #2

_____
_____
_____

Prayer Request #3

_____
_____
_____

<u>Prayer</u>
Lord, I come to You with these prayer requests. I pray that my desires align with Your will and that these prayers will be answered according to Your purpose. I thank You in advance for the victory and leave these requests with You. In Jesus' name I pray. Amen.

Letting God be in Control

Think about some things in your life that have fallen into place.

I remember a time when

_____
_____
_____

happened unexpectedly. After this event occurred, I felt as though this was meant or not meant to happen.

Was this event the result of your actions or did destiny take its course. What things did you do to influence this event?

_____
_____
_____

Was your influence good or bad? What will you do differently next time?

_____
_____
_____

Was your faith present during this event? _____
If no, what do you think the outcome may have been if your faith were present?

_____
_____
_____

Patches of Inspiration™ - Harvesting Your Success

The Power of Your Gift(s)

Think about the talents and gifts you have. List them here.
_____
_____
_____

How can your gifts be used to harvest your success?
_____
_____
_____

Reaping What You Sow; a Test of Giving

Here are some suggestions of how you can be a giver.
- ⇒ Volunteer in the community
- ⇒ Donate time
- ⇒ Donate money
- ⇒ Share knowledge
- ⇒ Take on leadership/ mentor roles

Are you a taker or giver? _____

Understanding that God blesses and rewards a giver, how can you give more to be a blessing to others?
_____
_____
_____

My Spiritual Harvest

Seeds	Roots	Weeds
Relationship with God	Relationship with God	Worry
Wisdom	Faith	Doubt
Knowledge	Gifts	Evil Spirits
Faith	Talents	Ignorance
Prayer	Life's Purpose	
	Prayer	
	Giving	

Notes _____
_____
_____
_____
_____
_____
_____
_____
_____
_____
_____
_____
_____
_____
_____
_____
_____
_____
_____

What is Meant for You is for You

Path to Success

Are you on your path to success? _____

In the box below, list the things you need to do to achieve your goals.

```
┌─────────────────────────────────┐
│         Goals to achieve        │
│                                 │
│   _____   │
│                                 │
│   _____   │
│                                 │
│   _____   │
│                                 │
│         Path to Success         │
└─────────────────────────────────┘
```

Forecast possible roadblocks that can obstruct your path to success. List them in the roadblocks below:

☐ ☐ ☐ ☐

Anticipate and remove possible roadblocks that can get on your path to success. The tool box contains items that can be used to remove the roadblocks you listed above.

```
┌─────────────────────────┐
│       **Toolbox**       │
│                         │
│          God            │
│         Prayer          │
│         Fasting         │
│        Meditation       │
│       Perseverance      │
│          Faith          │
└─────────────────────────┘
```

Your Destiny

Your life will take you through many phases. The phase of learning your purpose can be the most challenging because it often requires the removal of self from the equation. Success will come from doing what God has ordained you to do. Take the tools above and list how each will help fulfill your destiny.

Tool	How it will help
God	
Prayer	
Fasting	
Meditation	
Perseverance	
Faith	

My Destiny Harvest

Seeds	Roots	Weeds
Believe in your destiny	Exercise your natural gifts	Activities not in your purpose
Know your life's purpose	Exercise your talents	Not using your gifts
Sensitivity to your inner voice	Listen to your inner voice	Not using your talents
	Act in your purpose	

The Power of Leadership and Action

Playing Field of Life

What is the Right Playing Field?	Who are my mentors?
Who is my coach?	What resources do I need?

Think about a time when you took on a leadership role.

How did it make you feel?

_____
_____
_____

Did you maximize the opportunity and think about what type of influence you had on others?

_____
_____
_____

Looking back at it now, what would you have done differently?
___
___
___

My Leadership Harvest

Seeds	Roots	Weeds
Action Self motivation	Teamwork Positive influence on others Ability to pull others up Effective decision making Celebration of accomplishments	Procrastination Negative example to others Laziness

Notes ___
___
___
___
___
___
___
___
___
___
___
___

Does Your Image Work?

With respect to my image, others would say that I am

_____
_____
_____

Does this portray a positive or negative image? _____

How do I influence how people see me?

_____
_____
_____

My Uniqueness

Uniqueness is a gift from God because it differentiates you from everyone else. Different is okay; learn to embrace your uniqueness.

What makes you unique?
1. _____
2. _____
3. _____
4. _____
5. _____

How can you apply your uniqueness personally and professionally?

Character Seeds

Character seeds are things about you that can be planted in others. For example, joy, positive attitude, etc.

What are the seeds of your character?
1. _____
2. _____
3. _____
4. _____
5. _____

Are you planting positive or negative seeds? _____

<u>Prayer</u>
Lord, please help me to plant positive seeds and uplift Your kingdom. I pray that I am a light to the lives of all those I influence. In Jesus' name I pray. Amen.

Notes _____
_____
_____
_____
_____
_____
_____
_____
_____
_____
_____
_____

Patches of Inspiration™ - Harvesting Your Success

My Image Harvest

Seeds	Roots	Weeds
Positive image	Loving self	Negative image
High self esteem	Daily joy	Low self esteem
Belief in self	Self discovery	Validation from others
Spirit of joy	Good listening skills	Loud mouth
Originality		Settling on self
Validation of self		
Good character		

Notes _____

_____
_____
_____
_____
_____
_____
_____
_____
_____
_____
_____
_____
_____
_____
_____
_____

Building the right network is an important element towards achieving your goals and success.

Look at the diagram below and place the appropriate people and organizations in your network.

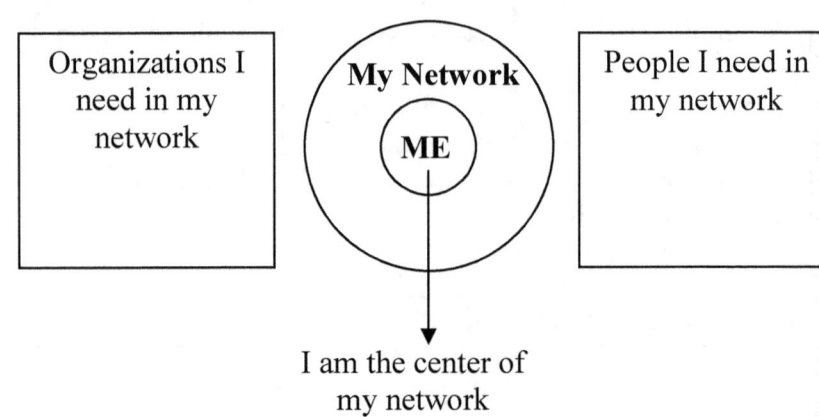

I am the center of my network

My Network Harvest

Seeds	Roots	Weeds
People of meaning	Meaningful relationships	Negative people
Symbolic figure of growth	Expanded territory	People who do not build you
Positive people		People who cannot help you grow
Building relationships		

Patches of Inspiration™ - Harvesting Your Success
Courage to Maneuver Obstacles and Challenges

Think about a time when you had to demonstrate courage.

How fearful were you to press forward during the challenge?
_____
_____
_____

Did you allow that fear to keep you from moving forward or did you press on?
_____
_____
_____

If you did press forward, how did you feel?
_____
_____
_____

If you did not press forward, how did you feel?
_____
_____
_____

What courage seeds do you need to plant?
_____
_____
_____

What courage roots do you need to develop?
_____
_____
_____

What courage weeds do you need to remove?
_____
_____
_____

<u>Prayer</u>
Lord, give me the courage to move forward during my times of fear. I understand that the godly walk courageously in the authority which has been given to us through Jesus Christ. Lord, I now plant my seeds of courage and walk boldly in the harvest that has been planted for me. In Jesus' name I pray. Amen.

My Courage Harvest

Seeds	Roots	Weeds
Courage	Ability to face challenges	Bad circumstances
Freedom	Ability to change circumstances	Turmoil
Movement	Pursuit	Fear
	Progress	Handicaps
		Obstacles
		Bondage and captivity

Notes _____
_____
_____
_____
_____
_____

State of Mind

The mind is a powerful object. Your mind is the most important part of your natural being because it has the ability to manifest greatness and defeat. To control your life, control your mind.

Success and ideas start with thoughts in the mind. Write your daydream in the callout box.

The weeds of negative thoughts and misery will try to enter your mind to prevent you from achieving the dream.

What seeds do you need to create your mental harvest?
_____
_____
_____

Reference the Roots of *My Mental Harvest* and fill in the blanks.

_____ Nourishment

Mental _____

Rationalization

Med _____

Day _____

My Mental Harvest

Seeds	Roots	Weeds
Positive thoughts	Mental nourishment	Negative thoughts
Joy	Mental guide	Misery
Peace	Rationalization	
Happiness	Meditation	
	Daydreaming	

Notes _____
_____
_____
_____
_____
_____
_____
_____
_____
_____
_____
_____
_____
_____
_____
_____
_____
_____
_____
_____
_____
_____

Owning Goals, Understanding Opportunity

Do you know where your open doors are? Behind every closed door is an open opportunity. List your open opportunities in the spaces below:

_____
_____

_____
_____

_____
_____

_____
_____

How can you use these open doors to achieve your goals?

_____
_____
_____
_____
_____
_____
_____
_____
_____

Sonie Bigbee

Think about three goals that you want to achieve.

Goal 1
My goal is _____. I would like to achieve this goal by _____. To achieve this goal I will need _____, _____, _____.

Goal 2
My goal is _____. I would like to achieve this goal by _____. To achieve this goal I will need _____, _____, _____.

Goal 3
My goal is _____. I would like to achieve this goal by _____. To achieve this goal I will need _____, _____, _____.

For each goal, complete the following:

	Goal 1	Goal 2	Goal 3
How much time will I allocate to achieving this goal?			
How committed am I to this goal?			
What is my risk and reward?			

My Opportunity Harvest

Seeds	Roots	Weeds
Goals	Opportunity	Fear
Positive image	Open doors	Negative image
Desire	Relationships	Laziness
Action	Strategy	Contentment

Notes

Align Your Pursuit with Your Opportunities

God's priorities:

_____
_____
_____
_____
_____
_____

My priorities:

_____
_____
_____
_____
_____
_____

Do my priorities align with the Word God? _____

How can I align my priorities and pursuit with the Word of God?

_____
_____
_____

Are the things I am pursuing filled with substance and meaning? _____

God's priorities include the following:
Him first
Salvation
Fellowship
Worship
Giving

Patches of Inspiration™ - Harvesting Your Success

Identify things you can pursue that align with the priorities of God.

_____
_____
_____

My Pursuit Harvest

Seeds	Roots	Weeds
Action	Alignment	Chasing the wrong things
Inspiration	Passion	Incompleteness
Drive		Selfish gain
Purpose		Dead works
Passion		

Notes _____
_____
_____
_____
_____
_____
_____
_____
_____
_____
_____
_____
_____
_____

Failure is Not So Bad

List a situation in which you made a mistake.

What was the mistake?
_____

Could you have prevented this mistake?
_____

How could you have prevented or minimized this mistake?
_____, _____
and _____.

What were the consequences of this mistake?
_____
_____
_____

Were you able to recover from this mistake? _____

How much time did it take you to recover from this mistake?
_____

Did you consider this mistake a failure? _____

Steps to minimize mistakes:
1. Surround yourself with smart people
2. Make wise decisions based on factual information
3. Be a consistent planner
4. Have a backup plan
5. Know when to change course

Patches of Inspiration™ - Harvesting Your Success

Using the mistake you listed above, fill in the blanks:

I could have surrounded myself with _____. I could have gathered my factual information from _____. My planning time should have lasted _____. I could have planned better by _____ and _____. I should have changed course before _____.

Go through this exercise after each mistake and use this learning as a platform for your future successes.

My Failure Harvest

Seeds	Roots	Weeds
Common sense Wisdom Support Solutions	Smart network Back up plan Ability to rise	Complications Bad path

Use the *Patches of Inspiration™ Success Model* (see page 134) to fill in the blanks.

Identify a _____ and evoke the _____ to go after it. Even if you face _____, make the _____ to get back in the game. Use _____ to press on despite the _____ or _____ and then bask in the glory of _____.

Seeds of Scripture

Courage
Matthew 14:27
Deuteronomy 31:6
Joshua 1:7-8
Psalm 27:14

Failure
Luke 22:32

Faith
Matthew 17:20
II Corinthian 5:7
Galatians 3:11
I Timothy 6:12
Hebrew 11:6

Goals
Philippians 3:14

Harvest
Matthew 9:37
Exodus 23:19
John 4:34-38

Image
Genesis 1:26

Leadership
Romans 8:14
Genesis 5:18
Matthew 2:6

Mind
Psalm 26:2

Romans 12:2
I Corinthian 2:16
Ephesians 4:23
Colossians 3:2
Romans 8:6

Mountain
Matthew 17:20
I Corinthian 13:2

Seeds
Matthew 13:24
Luke 8:6

Spirit
Galatians 5:16
Galatians 5:22
Ephesians 4:4

Success
Proverbs 2:7

Patches of Inspiration™ Success Model

Identify a **goal** and evoke the **desire** to go after it. Even if you face **failure**, make the **choice** to get back in the game. Use **courage** to press on despite **challenges** or **circumstances** and then bask in the glory of **success**.

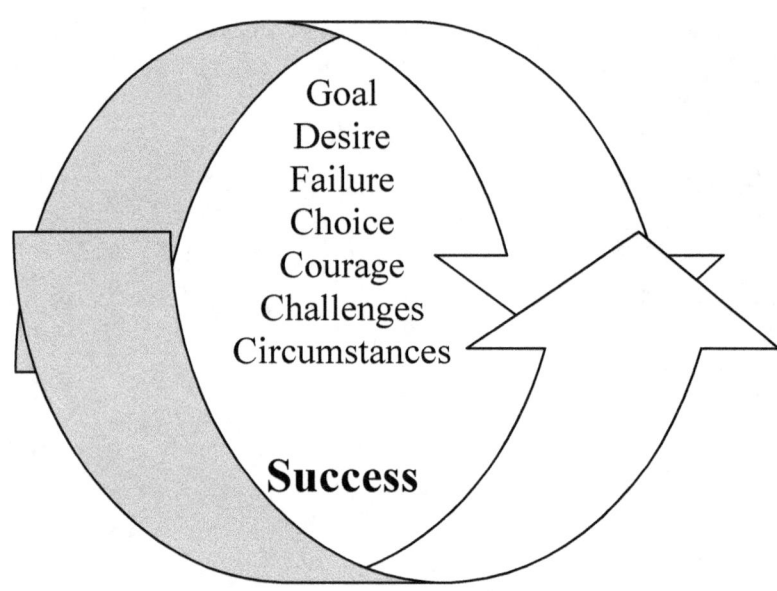

About Sonie Bigbee

Sonie Bigbee has been a force in Corporate America working for Fortune 500 companies in sales and management.

Taking on an entrepreneurial venture, she co-purchased an American Basketball Association franchise to become one of the first African-American women to hold ownership interest in a professional sports organization.

Sonie has been commissioned to teach others how to plant good seeds, develop needs and remove obstacles. Using an energetic approach, she motivates others to use their God-given gifts to achieve success.

Sonie obtained her B.S. from Wilberforce University and her MBA from University of Phoenix. She resides in Cincinnati, Ohio with her family.

Queen V Publishing
The Doorway to YOUR Destiny!

*Go thou and publish abroad
the kingdom of God.*
—Luke 9:60

We are a Christian contract publisher committed to transforming manuscripts into polished works of art. Queen V Publishing, a company of standard and integrity, offers an alternative that allows God's word in YOU to do what it was sent to do for OTHERS.

Visit the website for complete guidelines and the contract plan that best fits your literary goals and needs.

QueenVPublishing.net

We help experts master self-publishing!

Valerie L. Coleman
Queen V Publishing
Dayton, Ohio
937.307.0760
Info@PenoftheWriter.com

Other Queen V Titles

Are You Tired of Fighting Your Way to the Top?

Climbing the ladder of Corporate America may sometimes feel like you're moving sideways. In *I'm Here, Now What?*, Toni Perry Gillispie lets you know that you are not alone. Her expert guidance will help you choose the path that's best for you and encourage you to enjoy the journey.

Through life application, self-evaluations and sprinkles of affirmations, you will learn how to shatter the glass ceiling!

Available now at **TheInspiredWord.net!**
ISBN-13: 978-0-9817436-3-9
Retail: $9.95

Pen of the Writer

*Out of Ephraim was there a root of them against Amalek; after thee, Benjamin, among thy people; out of Machir came down governors, and out of Zebulun they that handle the **pen of the writer**.*
~ Judges 5:14

P_{en} O_{f the} W_{rit}ER

A Christian publishing company committed to using the writing pen as a weapon to fight the enemy and celebrate the good news of Christ Jesus.

Taking writers from pen to paper to published!
Passionate Pens
Write On! Workshop
Pen to Paper Literary Symposium
Literary Management & Consultation

POWER Awards

Pen of the Writer's commitment to recognizing inspirational authors and music artists for their contribution to the arts and entertainment industry

Pen of the Writer, LLC
Dayton, Ohio
937.307.0760
PenoftheWriter.com
info@PenoftheWriter.com

Patches of Inspiration™ - Harvesting Your Success

Prose, Rhythm and Praise

Your resource for clean entertainment

Prose, Rhythm and Praise provides management, promotions and booking for music artists, comedians, actors and more!

The *Prose, Rhythm and Praise* Internet talk show, hosted by Valerie Coleman, airs the first Thursday of every month at 9:00 pm EST.

Enjoy chats with national recording artists, best-selling authors and other experts in the Arts & Entertainment industry. Listen and participate during the live show at BlogTalkRadio.com/ChurchOhio.

To book clean entertainment for your event, contact us at Info@PenoftheWriter.com or 937.307.0760

ProseRhythmAndPraise.com

Blended Families An Anthology

A Black Christian Book Distributors and Christian Small Publishers Association Bestseller!

By Valerie L. Coleman
ISBN-13: 978-0-9786066-0-2

With divorce, single-parent households and family crises on the rise, many people are experiencing the tumultuous dynamics of blended or stepfamilies. Learn biblical principles and practical tools to help your family thrive. ***Blended Families An Anthology*** ministers to the needs of those hurting and crying out for answers.

We are **not** the Brady Bunch!

Tainted Mirror An Anthology

By Valerie L. Coleman
ISBN-13: 978-0-9786066-1-9

What's keeping you from your destiny? Whether restricted by prison walls, the influence of others or held hostage by self-inflicted limitations, captivity starts in the mind. We allow our thoughts to create virtual restrainers that stifle our dreams and hinder our purpose.

Based on I Corinthians 13:12, ***Tainted Mirror An Anthology*** offers stories of hope and healing to overcome the mental, physical and emotional strongholds that keep us from fulfilling our destiny.

Available on **Amazon.com, BlackCBD.com** and
PenoftheWriter.com

Patches of Inspiration™ - Harvesting Your Success

Order additional copies of

Patches of Inspiration™ - Harvesting Your Success
PO Box 1802
West Chester, Ohio 45071-1802
937.248.3394
PatchesofInspiration.com
Info@PatchesofInspiration.com

* * * * * * * * * * * * * * * * *

Please mail _____ copies of

Patches of Inspiration™ - Harvesting Your Success

_____
Name

_____
Address

_____
City / State / Zip

(_____)_____
Phone

_____
Email

Quantity	Price Per Book	Total
	$13.95	
Sales Tax (OH residents add $0.98 per book)		
Shipping ($2.99 first book, $0.99 each additional)		
Grand Total*(Payable to: Patches of Inspiration)		

* Certified check and money orders only

Get the entire *Patches of Inspiration*™ experience

Audio Collection

Patches of Inspiration™
Harvesting Workplace Success

Patches of Inspiration™
Harvesting Leadership Success

Patches of Inspiration™
Harvesting Daily Living Success

Patches of Inspiration™
Harvesting Spiritual Success

Patches of Inspiration™
Harvesting Small Business Success

Patches of Inspiration™
Harvesting Collegiate Success

Patches of Inspiration™
Harvesting Networking Success

Book your workshop or seminar today!
PatchesofInspiration.com

www.ingramcontent.com/pod-product-compliance
Lightning Source LLC
LaVergne TN
LVHW011714060526
838200LV00051B/2896